My Little Golden Book About

The First Moon Landing

By Chip Lovitt
Illustrated by Bryan Sims

The editors would like to thank Amie Gallagher, Planetarium Director, Raritan Valley Community College, for her assistance in the preparation of this book.

A GOLDEN BOOK • NEW YORK

Text copyright © 2019 by Penguin Random House LLC
Cover art and interior illustrations copyright © 2019 by Bryan Sims
All rights reserved. Published in the United States by Golden Books, an imprint of Random House Children's Books, a division of Penguin Random House LLC, 1745 Broadway, New York, NY 10019. Golden Books, A Golden Book, A Little Golden Book, the G colophon, and the distinctive gold spine are registered trademarks of Penguin Random House LLC.
rhcbooks.com
Educators and librarians, for a variety of teaching tools, visit us at
RHTeachersLibrarians.com
Library of Congress Control Number: 2018941303
ISBN 978-0-525-58007-2 (trade) — 978-0-525-58008-9 (ebook)
Printed in the United States of America
10 9 8 7 6 5

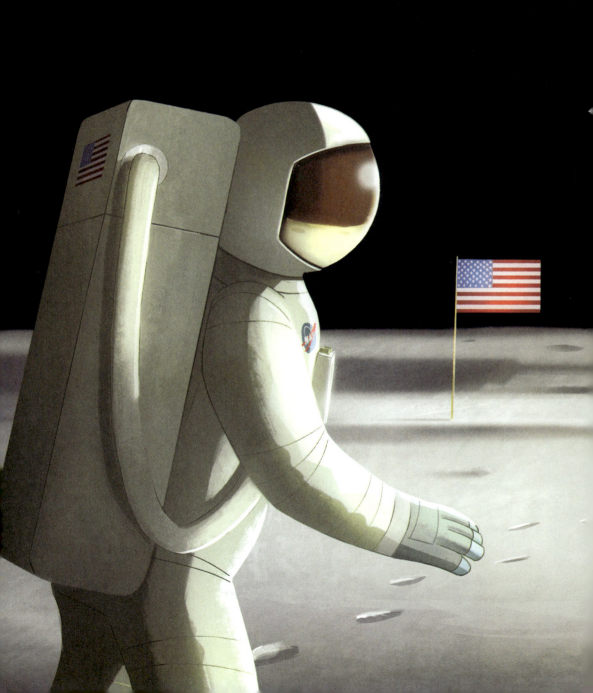

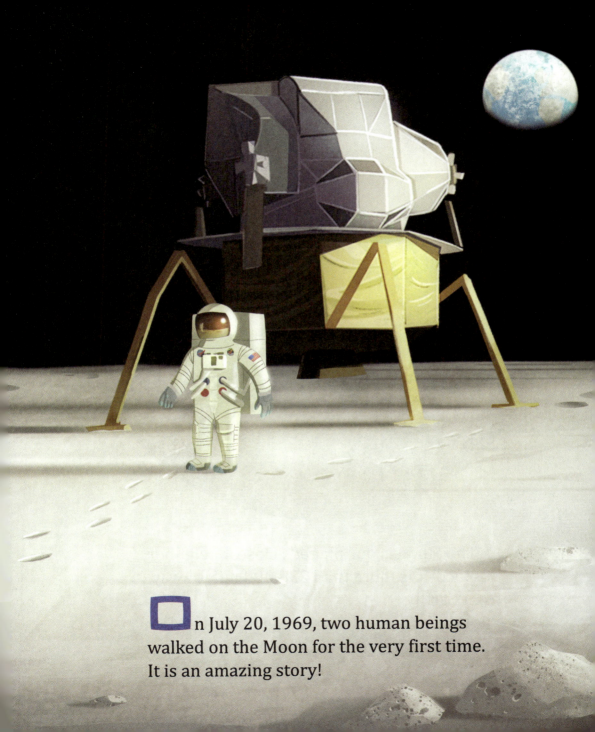

On July 20, 1969, two human beings walked on the Moon for the very first time. It is an amazing story!

    The Moon is our planet's closest neighbor in space. It is more than 238,000 miles away from Earth.

    Humans have always gazed up at the Moon. And we have always had the same question: "What's up there?"

Flying to the Moon seemed impossible until the 1960s. In 1961, President John F. Kennedy made a promise. He said America would land astronauts on the Moon—and return them safely to Earth—by 1970.

This trailblazing Moon mission would later be given a name: Apollo 11.

NASA
SATURN V

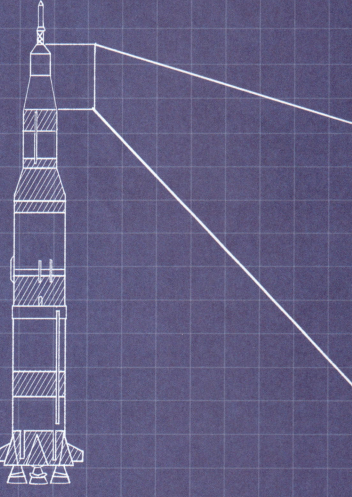

America's space agency is called NASA, which stands for National Aeronautics and Space Administration.

NASA would first need a powerful rocket to send the astronauts into space. They built a 363-foot rocket called *Saturn V*. It was as tall as a 36-story building!

Saturn V would carry a second unit, a command module called *Columbia.* It was shaped like a gumdrop and had a cabin for the astronauts. It would fly high above the Moon's surface while the astronauts did their moonwalk.

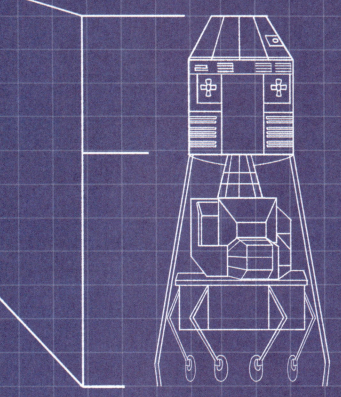

The third spacecraft was a lunar lander named *Eagle.* It looked like a giant insect. *Eagle* would drop down from the command module and land two astronauts on the Moon.

Three astronauts were chosen for Apollo 11. Neil Armstrong, Edwin "Buzz" Aldrin, and Michael Collins were experienced test pilots. They had already flown many dangerous missions in some of America's fastest jets.

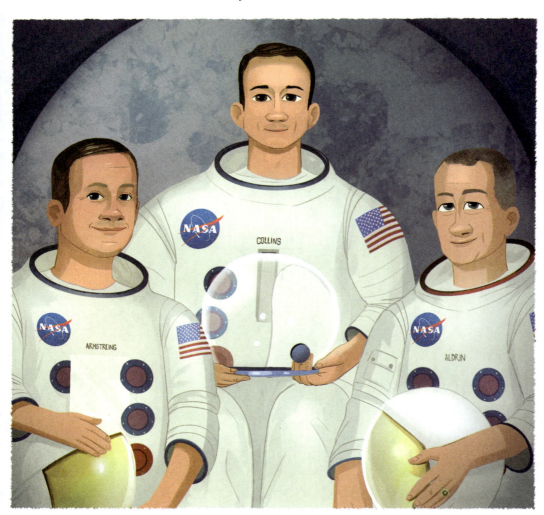

On the morning of July 16, 1969, the countdown began. "Ten, nine, eight, seven, six, five, four, three, two, one." Smoke and flames burst from the bottom of the rocket.

BLASTOFF!

Soon *Saturn V* was high above Earth. Faster and faster it flew: 6,000 miles per hour... then 15,000 miles per hour. The rocket quickly reached a speed of more than 24,000 miles per hour. That's more than six miles a second!

Once in space, *Saturn V* separated from the command module. Next, the command module separated from the lunar module. It turned around, then docked with the lunar module to join the hatches from the command module to the lunar module. Then the command module *Columbia* and the lunar module *Eagle* flew on toward the Moon.

Armstrong and Aldrin got into their space suits, then climbed into *Eagle.* Collins would stay in the command module, flying high above the Moon.

There is no air on the Moon. It can be both freezing cold and really hot. The astronauts' space suits would give them air to breathe. The suits would also keep them warm if they got too cold, or cool them off if they got too hot. Too much perspiration could fog up their helmets, and the astronauts would have no way to clean them while wearing them.

Their helmets also had radio gear for communicating with Collins and the NASA scientists back on Earth.

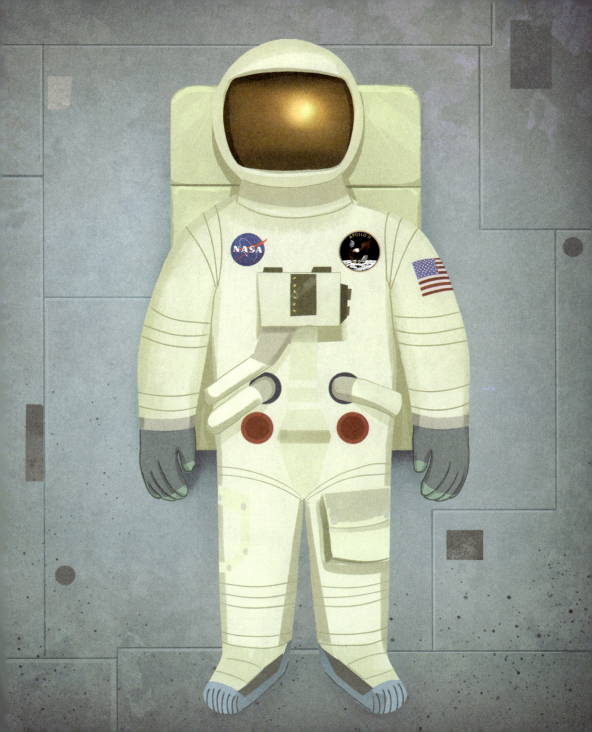

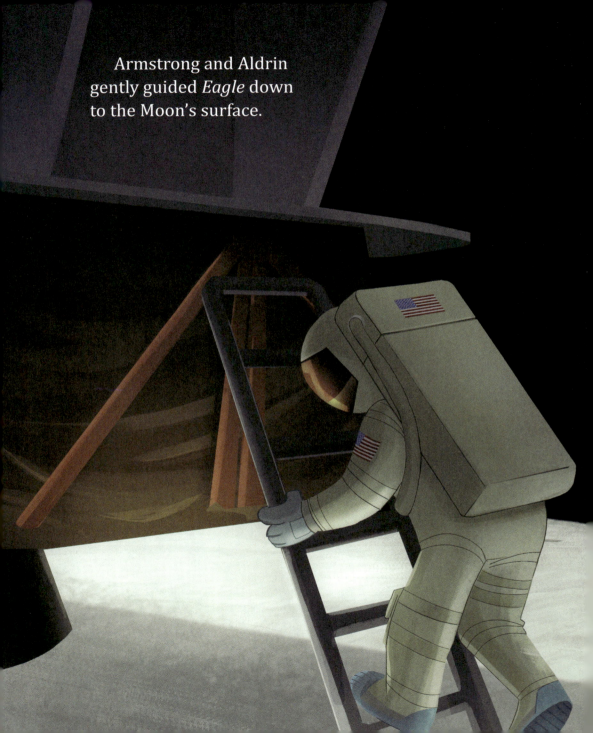
Armstrong and Aldrin gently guided *Eagle* down to the Moon's surface.

Six hours later, Armstrong made history as he climbed down a ladder and stepped onto the powdery surface of the Moon. Aldrin followed soon after, becoming the second person to walk on the Moon.

Armstrong sent this radio message back to Earth: "The *Eagle* has landed. . . . That's one small step for man, one giant leap for mankind."

Armstrong and Aldrin raised an American flag and left a plaque on the Moon's surface. The plaque reads "Here men from the planet Earth first set foot upon the Moon. July 1969 A.D. We came in peace for all mankind."

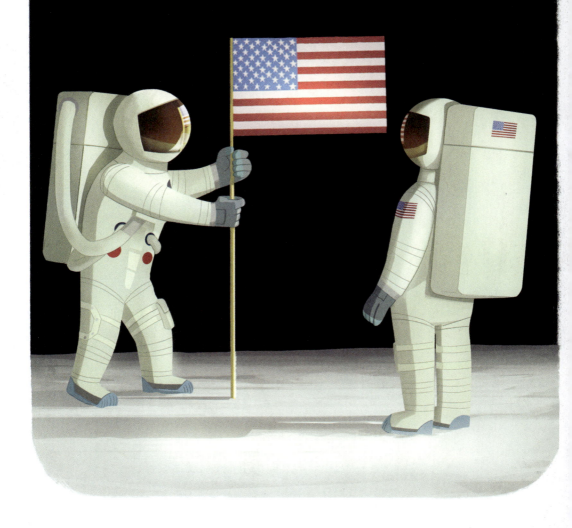

The astronauts spent nearly 22 hours on the Moon. They took photos and collected 40 pounds of Moon rocks. They also left something behind—the first human footprints on the Moon!

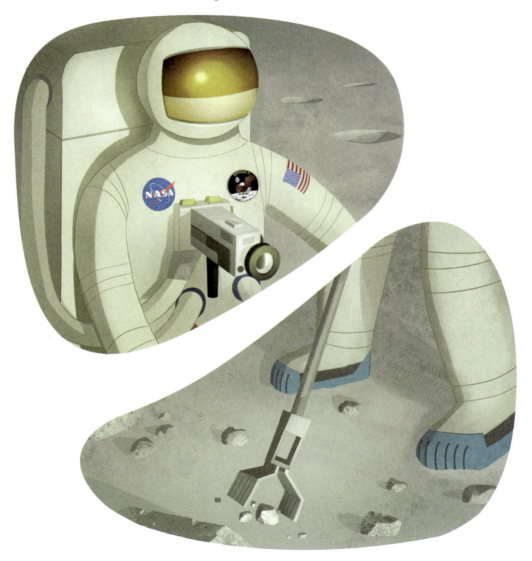

Soon it was time to return to the command module. Aldrin and Armstrong fired up *Eagle*'s engines and blasted off. Hours later, they were back with Collins in the command module. *Columbia* was heading home!

On July 24, 1969, *Columbia* splashed down in the Pacific Ocean. The USS *Hornet,* a U.S. Navy aircraft carrier, was there to pick up the astronauts.

Thanks to the astronauts' discoveries, scientists learned many things from the Apollo 11 mission. They came to believe that the Moon was once part of Earth until it broke off and flew into space long ago. Scientists also found evidence that the Moon has moonquakes, just as Earth has earthquakes.

The Moon landing was a remarkable feat. Armstrong, Aldrin, and Collins were America's newest heroes! Parades were held in their honor in New York, Chicago, and Los Angeles.

There would be five more NASA missions during which American astronauts would walk on the Moon. All of those brave astronauts followed in the footsteps of the amazing Apollo 11 crew.